Lofts

Author
Francisco Asensio

Publishing Director
Nacho Asensio

Texts
Laia Beltran

Design and Layout
Atrium Group

Translation
Matthew Connell

Production
Juanjo Rodríguez Novel

❮ ❯ **Copyright 2002 © Atrium Group**

Published by: Atrium Group de ediciones y publicaciones, S.L.
c/ Ganduxer, 112
08022 BARCELONE

Telf: +34 932 540 099
Fax: +34 932 118 139
e-mail: atrium@atriumgroup.org
www.atriumbooks.com

ISBN: 84-95692-67-8
Dep. Leg.: B-51042-03

Printed in Spain
Anman Gràfiques del Vallès, S.L

> Lofts

Contents

Lofts,
an appeal against uniformity

More than three decades have passed and architects and decorators continue to be surprised over and again by the ever-evolving design of the loft. Even though it might seem that everything has already been said, there are people out giving the wrench another turn and going beyond what has until a moment ago been unthinkable. The end result is almost always the same—a surprise—as the concept of the dwelling itself is renewed, rendered unique and inimitable.

As globalisation looms over mankind, threatening with it cultural and artistic homogeneity, risky wagers involving time and talent are always smiled upon. The lofts presented on these pages are an outstanding example of just this: though they follow similar guidelines, no two are exactly alike.

The loft is not a recent discovery. Since the early 1970s, artists and intellectuals have been emigrating from city centres in search of larger, more affordable buildings that would grant them space both to live and work. Over the years, this lifestyle-cum-philosophy caught on among liberal professionals and it was their growing interest that truly gave an impetus to the loft phenomenon. As ever-expanding cities envelop outlying neighbourhoods, that scarcely fifty years ago would have been considered distant, people have seen the need for revitalising and rethinking obsolete, abandoned spaces, before they fall prey—as many already have—to speculators. It is no coincidence, then, that most of the lofts examined here are to be found in antique warehouses, granaries and workshops in cities that have played major roles and continue to set trends in European cultural evolution: London, Paris, Antwerp and Amsterdam.

Fortunate too, is that lofts are not hung up on nationality. A loft is a reflection of its owner's personality, and, by extension, the architect and decorator whose time and talent went into designing it. These open, diaphanous spaces, incognizant of the tyranny of partitions, are no longer merely the privilege of artists and intellectuals: more and more devotees of the loft aesthetic, ready to break with convention, are starting work on their own lofts every day. Without a doubt, the sensation of knowing that the walls surrounding you hide decades—and in some case centuries—of history can only hold more meaning in these times of absolute homogenisation.

One of the great merits of this fin-de-siècle batch of lofts, in particular, is that out of respect for the past, their owners have made deliberate efforts to preserve original iron beams, brick walls, arched windows and wood floors. In new construction, materials like concrete, steel and stone accentuate the industrial character of these buildings, which have made an about-face in a very short time.

Perhaps the most over-the-top statement these lofts make is in their choice of décor: influences and references run from Japan to India, 1970s film to Cubism, or even the Italian baroque. Any period in history, any childhood memory or really any neurotic whimsy serves as a valid point of departure, just so long as it sets the imagination on a collision course with tradition. Styles come uninhibited, fusing and flowing together. The lofts scrutinised in this book provide a good example of just how far the renovation and design of these far-from-typical dwellings has progressed. A compilation of the best lofts found in four trend-setting cities should not, however, be understood as a mere catalogue. Quite to the contrary, it presents us with a unique opportunity to enjoy and contemplate other ways of living. Despite evident and needed differences, these lofts share common obsessions with space, natural light and the placement of quality over quantity. All said, with all their excesses and all their limitations, one can only conclude that there is something more, between intangible and magical, to these spaces, that draws the reader to delve into the pages of this book over and again. Go ahead—discover them for yourself.

LAIA BELTRAN

> In no rush

The argument that convinced the owners of this loft to buy it were its spectacular views over the centre of Antwerp: the Central Station, the Opera and St. James' Cathedral seem to be within grasp from both the windows and the terrace of this fourth floor loft. Additionally, the interior structure left room for architects and decorators' imagination to roam without requiring an involved renovation. To give an example, rather than dropping the ceiling to camouflage heating ducts, these simply became part of the decoration; just like the beams and columns, which in the end were merely given a coat of white paint.

Distributing spaces, which carefully conserve their original wood floors, followed a simple plan: from the entry hall one comes upon a large common space, which houses the dining room and living room. To one side, and separated from one another by partitions, are the kitchen and office. Beside the latter, but contained within a cube, is the bathroom. The upper floor became bedrooms, all of which have direct access to the terrace. Simplicity and good taste took care of the rest.

A small Japanese garden on the upper level terrace—hidden from guests—provides the perfect place for meditation.

With the exception of one painted black, the walls were painted a tone of ochre, whose exact shade varies throughout the day according to natural light.

Location: Antwerp, Belgium

Photographs: Bieke Claessen

The one black wall marks the entrance to the loft. In the foreground one can see the kitchen, which opens on to the dining room. Behind this are iron stairs that lead to the upper level.

This corner of the office was reserved for the cello.

In the bathroom, marble was used in place of wood. The large rectangular mirror reflects the glass blocks that hide the shower.

In the background, one can see the living room and the enormous windows that guarantee excellent views and a deluge of natural light.

› Sheer contrast

Who said that antiques and modern art were incompatible? This central-London loft shows that modernity need not turn up its nose at objects from yesteryear. The owner of this penthouse, situated in a rehabilitated antique warehouse, did not succumb to any particular aesthetic dogma and threw his entire collection of art into the mix. Working in a bank hadn't rendered him grey or unimaginative. And so you have it. He kept the original wood and limestone floors but didn't think twice about inserting a stainless steel kitchen and a thoroughly industrial metal stair. With these in place, he juxtaposed 1960s furniture, such as a chair and sofa designed by Robin Day for Hille, with baroque mirrors; a classical piano with contemporary Colorist canvases and the historic red brick walls with glass floors supported by iron beams.

Nevertheless, the culmination of this stylistic cocktail is its upper level. A room made entirely of glass, with a transparent floor and an Azco bubble chair suspended from its ceiling, it is surrounded by a terrace, paved in teak, fitted with a hydromassage pool and a row of pots planted with palms, bamboo and rosemary.

Artificial lighting stages a dialogue between light and shadow, further emphasising contrasts.

The bedroom is hidden behind a shaded glass panel to safeguard privacy.

Location: London, England

Photographs: Mathew Weinreb

The glass floor floods the lower level with natural light. ➤

The limestone hearth dominates the living room, one of the dwelling's most sober spaces in the dwelling. In the background, a small terrace replete with by plants.

Detail of the antique corner table, that never imagined itself resting against such a course brick wall.

Under the imposing steel staircase, the dining room table sits in harmony with six original leather chairs. In the foreground, a detail of the kitchen.

Industrial zen

An old warehouse that had belonged to French Railways was the place designer Thierry Watorek chose to make his home. With the inestimable assistance of designer Jean Paul Gaultier, he converted an overwhelmingly dull space into something almost magical, taking inspiration in Oriental motifs but careful not to overwhelm his home's industrial past. Four-metre ceilings allowed for the insertion of an L-shaped loft space, which takes full advantage of the available space. In this loft, however, contrasts are what grab you: in the living room, a white hearth is wrapped between furniture and flooring—both in iroko wood*. To one side of it was placed the dining room, and the kitchen was slid under the loft space. Atop it was built the office, accessed by a flight of wooden stairs. Further along one finds the master bedroom—a tatami-clad spot to relax—and at the end a bedroom for the clients' children.

A running theme through the loft's décor is the fusion of oriental motifs (paper lamps, prints…), objects found at flea markets (chairs, a filing cabinet, a window from a train…), and others found in the warehouse itself (a stove, metal lamps…). The result is an almost magical equilibrium between industrial rigidity and emotional, warm colours and sensual forms.

An antique oven rests beside a set of bookshelves, custom built into the cement pillars.

An eagerness to use recycled elements in the décor shows in the choice of furniture, window treatments, chairs and lamps—a tour de force of the imagination.

Architect: Thierry Watorek

Location: Argenteuil, Paris, France

Photographs: Emmanuel Barbe

An overall view of the loft taken from the living room. The kitchen is at the back and beside it, the dining room. The ceiling beams are wood and the enormous lamp hanging from it authentic.

A rest space was installed in the attic, complete with tatami mats. To the left: a view of the living room, distinguished by its plaster mantelpiece and an enormous hand-made paper lamp.

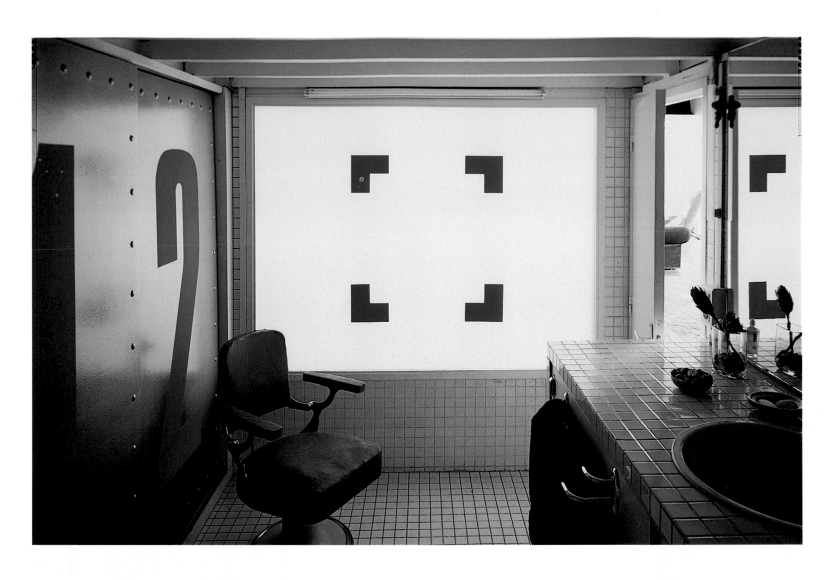

 A spinning barber's chair, bought at a flea market, was installed in the bathroom. Behind this is a translucent window, marked with red symbols, that can also be seen from the living room.

The master bedroom, decorated with an aviation motif and painted an intense blue, looks out upon the garden.

The table in the office was crafted in wood and painted a brilliant red, while the metal filing cabinet was purchased from a scrap merchant.

An aerial view of the kitchen, with its three orange leather stools.

A detail of the wooden bar in the kitchen, built by the owner to fit his own specifications. The rectangular window belonged to a train car.

» Zen equilibrium

Artist-designer André Martens' home, built in what had been a Jewish yeshiva, is an impressive two-storey loft where no detail was left up to chance. The kitchen, dining room and living room were all carved out of one single space on the ground floor. The master bedroom was separated from these common spaces by sliding panels, a technique repeated in the bathroom. This strategy was used again in other spaces and was a crucial inspiration at the moment of creating and delimiting new spaces, such as an art gallery. Additionally, all of the furnishings are movable, making rearranging them an easy task.

Martens adopted some Minimalist precepts for the design of the interior, but did not hesitate to use these spaces to place his own work on display, which, of course, he calls both workshop and home. He opted for white walls in order to emphasise natural light, and, for its unmatched elegance and calm. Light-toned wood, to transmit warmth, was chosen for the floor. Though they nearly pass unnoticed, some of the walls house built-in closets, which provide capacity for anything and everything without upsetting the Zen-like equilibrium that such an articulate décor had achieved.

A judicious combination of white tones, splashed with the black objects of the décor, breathes a harmonious air.

It is no coincidence that spaces end up serving as galleries for Martens to put his own work on display.

Architect: André Martens

Location: Amsterdam, the Netherlands

Photographs: Guy Obijn

In the foreground, the living room; and behind it, the master bedroom. Black wooden stairs lead to the loft space, lit by a unique series of white lamps. ➤

 Martens' work is present throughout the dwelling: dozens of his paintings, of all different sizes, hang from the walls.

The kitchen, hidden behind an American-style bar, is beneath the loft space. Facing it is the dining room, remarkable for a series of wooden cubes that fuse the function of table and chairs into one singular object.

Two imposing metal easels dominate the studio. The bathroom owes its Zen nature to its mix of materials.

An inviting corner, perfect to relax with a book, guarded over by a lamp reminiscent of a film set.

The warmth of wood was chosen to flesh out the rectilinear design of the kitchen.

Industrial sensibility

Behind this building's sober brick façade is much more history than one could possibly imagine at first sight. Pulleys, used to hoist cargo up and down, evidence its initial use as a warehouse. During the Second World War it served as a granary, only later to return to its original function—up until being converted into private flats. The attic floor, in particular, was transformed into a well-appointed loft with beautiful views of the city of Antwerp. Though footprints of the past remain—iron columns, an odd brick wall painted white, and the ceiling's wooden beams—the rest is a different story.

Though he did not wish to renounce the building's industrial origins, the loft's owner painstakingly remodelled the interior in search of the aesthetic equilibrium that he felt would cause rooms, sharing a common space, to coalesce. The perfect formula was the skilful combination of designer furniture and details crafted in steel—among them the stairs, railing and living room fireplace—whose chilliness is offset by the wood floor, white walls and rigorous use of lighting.

To create more space, an upper level was built atop the kitchen and dining room. Here one finds the work area.

Plants, used in the living room décor, soften the imposing presence of the steel chimney.

Architect: Nicolas Vanderhaeghen

Location: Antwerp, Belgium

Photographs: Guy Obijn / Stefan Petkov

From the living room, one can see the kitchen, dining room and office, situated on the upper level. The bookshelves and chairs are by Philippe Starck.

Iron columns recall the building's industrial origins. The dining room lamp is a masterwork of the imagination.

The living room unfolds around an enormous steel fireplace and chimney, crowned with a neon halo.

From the loft space one can make out the majestic living room, shaped by two sofas, two armchairs and a coffee table with extendable leaves.

Multipurpose spaces

This loft takes up no less than three floors of a Victorian-era school located in Battersea. Although it was initially conceived of strictly as being a dwelling, in the end it came to house one of the clients' businesses as well: a pioneering project for the 1990s in the adaptation of space for both personal and professional use. Architect Mark Guard opted for a combination of inviting, smaller spaces with large, open areas, housing different spaces at different levels off the floor. He was thus able to justify, for example, a guest bedroom that opens on to the immense living room.

One of Guard's other signature touches was the use of sliding doors both to partition rooms and simultaneously act as bastions of vivid colour, breaking the monotony of the colour white. Minimalist tendencies inspired many details in the design of the interior, and, as an anecdote from the past, the original brick walls of the college were kept intact, albeit concealed under a thick coat of white paint.

One of the clients set up his own business on the ground floor of the building: an antique poster restoration studio.

Even though the supremacy of the colour white is indisputable, the exacting selection of décor bestowed the flat with an extensive palette of colours.

Architect: Mark Guard

Location: Battersea, London, England

Photographs: Mathew Weinreb

Free-standing, wooden stairs cased in steel connect the living room with the guestbedroom above.

∧ The bed, emulating a Japanese tatami, lounges carelessly in the centre of the master bedroom. An addiction to feng shui?

Above: Half-open Venetian blinds allow a sneak glance at one of the bathrooms.
Below: Ron Arad chairs with curved legs and plastic bodies were chosen for the
dining room area, decorated with a saddle.

» Structure with style

When they visited this former locksmith's workshop for the first time, the owners of this loft were left breathless. Proof of its original purpose lay in an iron staircase connecting the two levels and its imposing industrial lamps. Nonetheless, the most surprising detail was the space reserved for the workshop's office: situated on the upper level, it conserved its glass walls as well as a set of enormous filing cabinets built into the wall.

Presented with such a panorama, the owners decided to modify the original structure as little as possible, limiting themselves to giving walls and ceilings a fresh coat of white paint. For its warmth, they chose a light-toned parquet for the floor, so that it would contrast with the cold iron. Large windows were opened into the walls of the first floor to act in unison with the skylights, letting in light. The final choice was for designer furniture, and, naturally, the unmistakable elegance of the colour white. The clients' present to themselves was the terrace, where white was switched for ochre on the walls. Multi-coloured tiles were chosen to pave the terrace to match the terracotta floor in the kitchen. A wooden table and chairs, together with some candles and flowerpots, are the terrace's sole ornamentation.

The multi-coloured tiles on the terrace and those in the kitchen were imported from Morocco.

Iron beams and columns also form part of the original structure of the workshop.

Location: Paris, France

Photographs: Emmanuel Barbe

A view of the living room from the kitchen, whose multi-coloured tiles jump out at the eye. The stools are crafted in leather and steel. »

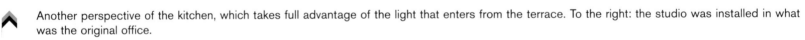
Another perspective of the kitchen, which takes full advantage of the light that enters from the terrace. To the right: the studio was installed in what was the original office.

Two glass-block panels separate the master bedroom from the common areas. In the bedroom, light filters in through the two skylights that were installed in the roof.

At one end of the living room, another set of iron stairs leads to the bedrooms on the upper level. To the left one can see part of the dining room, with its impressive Le Corbusier table.

The bar has two functions: it outlines the space of the kitchen and serves as a table for solo meals.

A set of white sofas and armchairs around a wooden coffee table, together with the original side tables, make for an elegant living room.

> Play ball!

Without a doubt one can say that the owner of this building, which had held a bank office, was ready for fun when he decided to convert it into his new home. The conversion from office to dwelling required numerous structural changes, but the most valuable elements of the structure were retained, such as the energetic stone(?) beams that cross and prop up the living room ceiling. Something else the client managed to hold on to was the original armoured door to the bank's vault, which was transformed into the access to the kitchen! Imagination was left to run wild yet again in the bathroom, nestled between glass-block walls. The wood flooring used throughout the loft was here replaced by something entirely different: the floor was paved with hundreds of smooth stones taken from a beach, from between which emerge the standard fixtures of any bathroom—lavatory, toilet and tub.

The master bedroom is hidden behind a 4 x 6-metre revolving door, which, when closed, serves as a wall. Netting drapes over the bed and the problem of closet space was resolved in a most original manner: twelve compartments for storage were built in the wall above space to put away clothing and shoes.

Details reveal most clearly the owner's penchant for recycling. A perfect example of this: the five wooden armchairs in the living room, rescued from an old cinema.

Immense, industrial windows unabashedly flood the dwelling with natural light.

Architect: Paul De Bruyn

Location: Amsterdam, the Netherlands

Photographs: Guy Obijn

Thanks to the light tones of the wood floor and the white of the walls, a sensation of spaciousness is felt throughout the loft. >

The pinball machine, opposite the living room, inevitably proves itself to be an irresistible draw. And, amazingly, it works!

The imposing bathtub, raised up on stainless steel feet, is the pièce de résistance of the bathroom.

The vault door was kept intact and the living room floor installed around it. Polished concrete was chosen for the kitchen floor.

» Home gym

An awe-inspiring structure of iron staircases and catwalks connects the three floors of this loft, which played home originally to a small school. Of its past, though, merely its walls remain, as the owner—on his quest for the perfect space—decided to otherwise completely remodel the interior so it would be wide open, peaceful and flooded with light. Taking advantage of the catwalks and stairs, he achieved a sensation of freedom and open space far-flung from the tyrannical monotony of the traditional scheme of four-walled rooms.

Though spaces are distributed along the lines of a rather traditional arrangement, it turns out to be a very practical scheme: the ground floor was split into a living room and game room, which was then decorated with the owner's personal collection of Coca-Cola posters and cut-outs from the 1950s. For the living room décor, however, he opted for African masks and sculpture, along with sporting imagery, each representing another of his great passions. The second floor was reserved for the kitchen, dining room and bathroom; and the top floor, the bedrooms and private gym, a hotch-potch of fitness machines.

The owner's weakness for pinball machines is rather obvious: on the ground floor alone he installed three of them.

The old courtyard is now a beautiful interior garden that doubles as a terrace.

Location: Antwerp, Belgium

Photographs: Guy Obijn

The different levels of the loft are interconnected by stairs and catwalks. In the background, the owner's private gym.

A spiral iron stair connects the ground floor with the first. The images from comic books were painted directly onto the wall. To the right: the vaguely ethnic dining room table and chairs, lost amidst a swarm of sport photographs.

The kitchen, finished in a combination of natural-finished wood and wood painted black, was installed beneath an iron structure and paved with tiles.

Another view of the gymnasium, with its fitness equipment picking up practically every hue of the rainbow. Another corner houses a worktable.

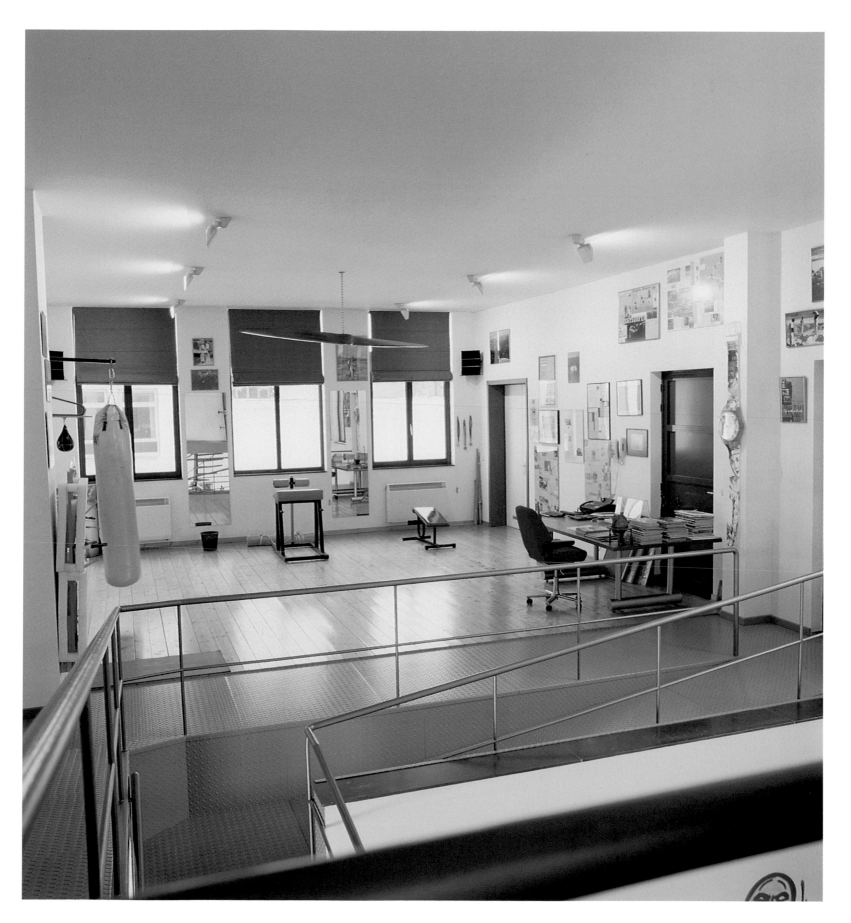

> And there was light

The attic floor of an old wool warehouse built in Clerkenwell in the fifties provided architect Fiona Naylor with the perfect excuse to transform a dark space into an open loft, flooded with light. The original lift of the warehouse leads directly to the dwelling, smartly arranged about the central core, yielding an immense living room presided over by a hearth built into the wall. To make the most of the building's solid mass, a transparent pavilion was built above the main floor to provide a space for reading. A terrace, spectacularly endowed with views, stretches around this glass cube, crowning the building.

The use of unembellished materials, such as steel, American oak in the floor and concrete paving, endow this space with quality, defining severe lines best characterised as sober and elegant. Despite a notable Bauhaus influence and the omnipresent white of the walls, flirtations with Minimalism are kept to these, mere flirtations, as the inspired choice of furnishings forges a character far too distinct to be lumped into traditional categories.

To keep radiators from upsetting the equilibrium, a radiant heating system was installed beneath the floor.

The contrast between concrete and wooden slats in the floor, embellished by natural light, conveys a unique warmth to the dwelling.

Architect: Fiona Naylor

Location: London, England

Photographs: Mathew Weinreb

Glass railings filter natural light from the large windows on the upper level down to the main areas of the dwelling. Lacquered MDF shelving echoes the straight lines of the composition.

The living room is divided into two clearly distinct environments. In the foreground, chairs designed by Gerrit Rietveld.

The terrace, equipped with hammocks and a table, stretches around the entire upper level.

In the master bedroom wardrobes and bureaux have been replaced by a bar to hang clothes and a filing cabinet, respectively.

The kitchen backs into the dining room, an elevated platform of American oak separating the two at floor level.

A chessboard, framed by two designer chairs, roosts in an intimate corner of the upper level.

Art and religion

Seiichiro Shimamura, president of a Japanese textile company, fell victim to Paris' charm: it was there that he unveiled N° 44, his own clothing boutique, and there that he decided to call home. The chosen spot was a two-storey locale located along the back edge of a courtyard that, in its day, had housed a printing press. Taking advantage of its high ceilings and diaphanousness, Shimamura created a made-to-measure temple: on the ground floor, ceilings, floors and walls were painted an immaculate white and on the upper level the original oak floor restored. Save for in the kitchen, which he equipped with the latest technology, and the functional, practical bathroom, Shimamura chose to eliminate any and all architectural barriers that could possibly separate the dwelling's spaces from one another, or, as he saw it, a body from its soul. In the living room, on the ground floor, crosses and candelabras mingle with antique tables and chairs.

This then shares space with the kitchen and envelops the dining room. Above, separated by imaginary lines, are a bedroom, an area to relax and another space for work. An air of mysticism, accentuated by Shimamura's obsession with lighting his home—as though it were a church—simply and succinctly, lingers throughout.

The stairs are lit by the same lights used to illuminate staircases in theatres and cinemas.

Lamps have been replaced by small task lights, and, of course, candles.

Location: Paris, France

Photographs: Emmanuel Barbe

The living room is decorated with objects used in religious liturgy, whose presence is accented by the coats of white vinyl paint on the walls and floor.

The living room from another perspective. To the right: the hydromassage bathtub in the white-walled, chocolate-brown-tiled bathroom.

The work area, bedroom and a space to relax are fused together on the upper level. A cube, painted white, encloses the bathroom.

Skylights ensure natural light. The floor shows its original, restored oak boards. The birdcage, a classic motif in Japanese decoration, was purchased from a Paris antiquarian.

The kitchen reflects the owner's desire for technological functionality, as much as in its design as in the appliances that fill it. The old wooden chairs, of course, are the exception that proves the rule.

A diamond in the rough

This building, which in its day was a diamond-cutter's workshop and later, a technical school, is found in one of Amsterdam's historically Jewish neighbourhoods. The clients opted for minimal modification of the original structure—a genuine diamond in the rough—building a loft space primarily to mitigate the ground floor's seven-metre ceilings. The result is an impeccable series of spaces, some open, others hidden, linked by the common denominator of an eclectic décor, white walls and the light tones of the wood floor.

The main volume is divided between the kitchen, living room and dining room. In the latter there was somehow room for a mantelpiece designed by Picasso, a designer coatstand, an old pianola and a piece by Jan Wolker. Fused together in the other main area are the master bedroom and a workspace, dominated by a large white wooden bookcase.

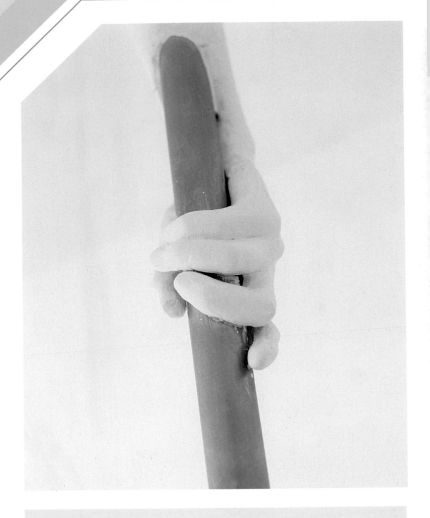

In the ceiling above the loft space, two plaster hands grab at a pair of iron tubes which integrate into the structure of the railing.

The combination of restored antiques with other, avant-garde pieces is repeated, elegantly, throughout the loft.

Location: Amsterdam, the Netherlands

Photographs: Jo Jetten

The most daring aspect of the otherwise humble bathroom are its walls, painted a brilliant red.

The focus of the dining room is an antique mantelpiece, designed by Picasso, as well as a rectangular marble table. The one-time shop display case—replete with drawers—was bought from an antiquarian in Belgium.

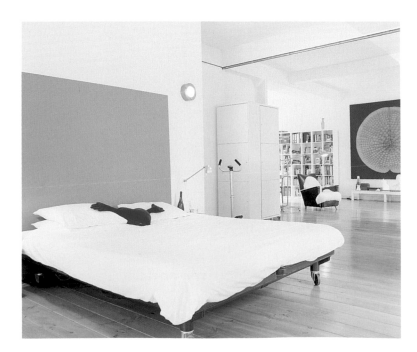

The master bedroom opens on to the living room. Wheels make moving the bed an easy task.

A dried lotus leaf, mounted on the wall, adorns one corner of the living room, behind an austere designer black leather armchair.

The weight of iron

The central Le Globe department stores, founded in 1886, were for years a veritable Antwerp institution. For this reason architect Jo Peeters undertook the renovation of the aged building deferentially, taking great pains in particular over preserving the original façade. The renovation of the interior, however, was virtually absolute, the original layout giving way to 25 lofts. In one of these, a 320-square-metre space on the attic floor, the owner delimited rooms in an otherwise open, diaphanous space by simply building two partitions. One of these, painted blue, hides the bathroom and various closets, while the other, painted an intense yellow, keeps the kitchen from view.

The iron columns, wooden beams and some brick walls recall the industrial character of the dwelling, which continues to be lit by ample, large windows. The common space was divided between the living room and dining room, both of which also additionally house different sub-environments, such as a reading area and another for play. While the décor of the two bedrooms, separated by sliding doors, sounds markedly Oriental notes, wooden and wicker furniture dominate the rest of the loft, their lightness providing a clever contrast to the gravity of the beams and iron columns.

Despite its proximity to the railway station, double-glazing insulates this loft from bothersome sounds.

Treated stone was used for the floor throughout except for in the bedrooms and the bath, which were clad in chestnut.

Architect: Jo Peeters

Location: Antwerp, Belgium

Photographs: Guy Obijn

In the foreground, adjacent to the kitchen, a round table and some chairs, forming part of the dining room. In the background, the guest dining room and to the right, the ample living room.

Functionality took first priority in the kitchen. The guest dining room centres on a long wooden table, seconded by chairs crafted in iron and wicker.

The choice of two antique lavatories was key to achieving the retro feel of the bathroom.

All of the kitchen utensils are organised and put neatly away. The stone counter comes from Belgium.

> Northern accent

The L-shaped plan of an antique warehouse in London, along with its iron columns and beams painted white, was kept intact to give rise to an austere, minimally ornamented loft. The large, slightly rounded stone windows, well distributed about the building, guarantee ample light throughout. Polished oak boards were laid down on the floor, their warmth in contrast to the cold antique brick walls.

In keeping with his Scandinavian origins, the client pushed for quality furniture. Though he chose few pieces, all of them are well designed and well suited to the space. This label fits the large dining room table designed in chestnut by Mark Gabbitas as well as the solid kitchen furniture. Black sofas, their straight lines drawn from 1950s designs, were placed in the living room along with original hammocks. The master bedroom, half-hidden behind a ruddy brick wall, is distinguished by its simplicity and whiteness—in sharp contrast to the black slate decorating the adjacent bathroom.

Black wooden doors across from the kitchen conceal cupboards that camouflage electric appliances at the same time they provide storage space.

The client's zest for total design is evident even in the smallest of details: the fruit basket, the dustbin, candles…

Location: London, England

Photographs: Mathew Weinreb

In the foreground, the impressive dining room table, adjacent to the kitchen. Behind it, four columns define the living room. >

Two black sofas, one across from the other, dominate the living room—itself an array of hammocks of all shapes and sizes. To the right, shelves hold books by the armful.

The austerity of the bathroom is even further accentuated by its slate floor and black bathtub.

In one corner of the living room, a hammock hung from an original wooden frame looks ready to provoke relaxation and idleness.

The bathroom's sliding door, painted an intense shade of red, is used here as a wall from which hang shelves for a veritable collection of toiletries.

> In the nude

The most likely fate for a 10,000-metre abandoned factory in the Bagnolet suburbs is, of course, to end up loft apartments. And this is exactly what happened with this building, blessed with the extra advantage of opening onto a common courtyard. Respecting the original structure, the owners decided to arrange spaces in small groups, leaving entire areas devoid of anything. The office was built on the ground floor, right beside the hall, and the kitchen hidden behind a white wall.

The dining room is an artfully simple space, and the living room is composed of a sofa and chairs draped in white sheets. The enormous skylight in the ceiling and the sizeable glazed area of the wall at the entry guarantee adequate natural light. A die-cast steel stair was kept to serve as access to the upper level. This space, then, was divided between a rather unconventional bathroom and several bedrooms.

The loft's polished concrete floor, white walls and wooden furnishings make for a living space with a lively personality, despite its stark walls and constant feeling of emptiness. After all, the owners' firm stance against gratuitous exhibitionism is made more than clear.

The storage area was housed in several compartments next to the living room and kept from view by curtains.

Most of the furnishings were acquired at flea markets and restored by the owners themselves.

Location: Bagnolet, Paris, France

Photographs: Laurent Teisseire

The bathtub is integrated into a wooden platform, to the right of which a sliding door hides a traditional shower. The taps of both the lavatory and the bathtub bring garden fixtures to mind. >

The chairs and sofas in the living room were covered with white sheets, as though awaiting an impending move. The dining room, formed by a square table and three chairs, is found to the right. The kitchen was hidden behind the white wall.

A view of the inside of the kitchen, situated beneath the metal stairs that lead to the attic. Here one finds the only paintings hung on any wall throughout the entire loft.

All of the furniture in the office (chair, tables and filing cabinet) was rescued from flea markets and restored with this space in mind.

> Colonial accents

The historic centre of Amsterdam houses numerous buildings which, in their day, served as warehouses, factories, workshops and depots. In addition to their excellent location, their enormous dimensions and high ceilings convert these buildings into objects of desire for all those dreaming of a loft of their own. When designing this flat, on the intermediary floor of an old warehouse, the owners wanted for its spaces to open into one another, avoiding as much as possible the construction of partitions or sliding doors. Small sets of stairs and white columns were used to separate and define different areas, enlivening the loft with a unique rhythm.

To better articulate the spaces of the loft, the original hall was eliminated and in its place built a large living room—peppered, nevertheless, with smaller spaces. A rail-less stair leads to the kitchen and dining room on the upper level, while the bedrooms and bathrooms key into one side of the living room. The décor is a nonchalant mélange of designer furniture (Le Corbusier), antiques, paintings and exotic flourishes, such as a zebra-hide rug. The result is a comfortable and relaxed atmosphere, with a marked colonial accent—seconded by the earth tones in objets d'art and furniture.

The terrace was fitted with an ensemble of wooden table and chairs, as well as a huge white umbrella to shield sunlight.

Wood floors and white walls are this loft's hallmark.

An overall view of the living room. The sofas and armchairs, designed by Le Corbusier, mark off an area separate from the rest of the loft. From the walls hang impressive works of art. >

Location: Amsterdam, the Netherlands

Photographs: Guy Obijn

Antiques and works of art have their spot in every corner of the home.

From this welcoming corner of the living room, occupied by a corner settee upholstered in mauve velvet and accompanied by orange cushions, one's gaze floats up to the dining room, situated on the upper level.

An impressive set of steals the scene in the reading area, though the zebra skin, wide-screen TV and stairs leading to kitchen are hardly demure.

Dark blue furnishings predominate in the kitchen, contrasting with the aluminium appliances. Glassware is kept inside the auxiliary workbench.

The bathroom glows, what with its white walls, wooden furniture and black border details and accessories.

This sculpture, inspired by African warriors, is a work of artist Rhonda Zwillinger.

» Absolute calm

Renovating an old warehouse to make it into a sober and functional dwelling presented architect Christel Peeters with a sizeable challenge. This veritable sea-change implied searching for something that would synthesise the spirit of a loft—synonymous with open, interconnected spaces—with the clients' demand for privacy in others. Peeters' solution was both inventive and practical: she built two enormous cubes to be visible from any corner of the loft, one of which houses the master bedroom and jacuzzi, while the other is used as a dressing room and guest bedroom. Basic materials used throughout exude serenity: concrete floors were left bare and the two cubes' walls and doors were dressed in walnut.

The ceiling and the remainder of the walls were painted a surface white to accentuate the building's industrial origins. The resulting open space was distributed between the kitchen—complete with a spectacular five-metre-long oak table—the living room and a simple office. The décor makes a statement of the clients' passion for animal-print chairs and rugs, complemented by a rigorous selection of furniture in black.

Natural light flows in through large windows, another nod to this loft's industrial past.

A full array of closets was built into the side of one of the cubes.

Architect: Christel Peeters

Location: Antwerp, Belgium

Photographs: Guy Obijn

The walnut decorating the cubes' walls is responsible for the loft's feeling of calm. Located further behind the writing desk are the master bedroom and the jacuzzi.

A row of built-in closets occupies one of the cube's walls. Stairs lead to a loft space, into which was nestled a guest bedroom.

Due to its length, the oak kitchen table is often used for formal dining.

The office could not be simpler: a designer table in glass and steel and a leopard-skin chair.

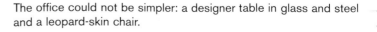

 The jacuzzi, bathroom and master bedroom are all fused into one space, dominated by the colour white. An Oriental-style chair is the only decoration.

The living room follows the same slogan as the rest of the loft: sobriety and space to spare.

A rhythm of curves

The owner of this loft is a stockbroker who was looking for a brightly-lit and welcoming space to live. The L-shaped floor plan of this antique warehouse offered the architect a multitude of ways to grant his client's wishes: generous windows graced all three wings of the dwelling and the space acquired a sensual roundness thanks to the interplay of curves and columns. A curving wall, imitating the path taken by a railway, is the structure that sets the rhythm of the loft: it originates in the hall—a long passage combining brick and stone—and opens up into the common area.

The kitchen is found at the front of the dwelling, dominated by an impressive bar made from American cherry in the shape of a half-moon. The living room, fitted with two sofas upholstered in brilliant blue velvet, is situated at the back. Beside it, separated by one sole column, is the dining room, whose furnishings are limited to a table and matching benches designed in oak by Mark Gabbitas.

Plants and bouquets of flowers, found throughout the house, add a natural touch to the décor.

Lighting, whether incandescent, halogen or fluorescent, provides the architect a useful tool with which to highlight different areas of the dwelling.

Location: London, England

Photographs: Mathew Weinreb

The luminosity of the common area is partly due to the use of light-coloured woods, such as birch, in the floor panels.

Noteworthy in the master bedroom—which juxtaposes white walls against the original brick—is the Minimalist furniture crafted out of cherry.

The traditional radiator has been replaced by a spiral model, hung and illuminated as though it were a work of art.

In the bathroom, black mosaic tiles were used for the shower niche, stainless steel for the sink, wood on the floor and marble for the bathtub.

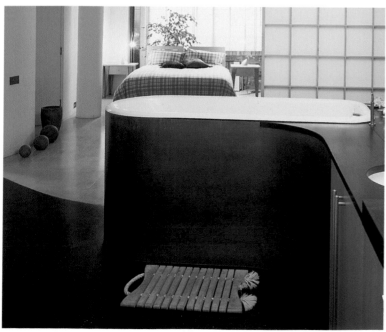

» Intelligent solutions

Synthesising the needs of a family with those of two professionals was the main challenge architects Caroline Béart and Frédéric Bogino faced when redesigning a 200-square-metre space to simultaneously serve as their home and two independent offices. Making it even more difficult, they were steadfast in their desire to maintain the spirit of liberty that the concept of a loft meant to them. The solution came in the form of building a long vestibule to snake through the entire flat and connect spaces with one another.

They hid closets by building them into its walls, as well as sliding doors that allow them to instantaneously reconfigure spaces as they need to. This hall, designed as though it were a street, originates in the entry and passes through three rooms, two bathrooms and a dressing room, reaching its terminus in an ample common area, which holds the living room, dining room and kitchen. To the side, a small library, supported by an iron column, defines the entry to the two studios. Pieces in quality hardwoods typify the décor, as well as designer furniture and a few resolute pieces of art.

The colour black was utilised exclusively on the iron columns, the office windows and picked up in the piano and a few pieces of furniture.

Floors, doors and shelves are finished in oak for the unique warmth it transmits.

Architect: Caroline Béart y Frédéric Bogino

Location: Paris, France

Photographs: Laurent Teisseire

Where the vestibule enters all of the rooms. In the background, all of the common areas were grouped together in one undivided space.

A row of windows separates the two studios from the rest of the loft.

The kitchen, completely open to the living room, elegantly combines wood and steel, avoiding the presence of cabinets.

A black leather sofa and several chestnut-coloured leather chairs were chosen for the living room. Below: a detail of the unique lamp and end table in one.

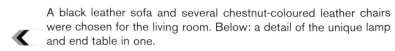

 In the foreground one can make out the two studio. Behind them, the dining room table and the piano.

A detail of the iron column that marks the entrance to the two offices.

While the chattering of children and the school bell are only distant memories, the majestic air of this building, which years ago had served as a primary school, remains unaltered. The space that held two classrooms and a long corridor was converted into a spacious and light-filled loft, opening the resulting spaces as much as possible to the entrance of natural light. The redesign of the flat respected the original steel beams and columns, painting them, however, a metallic blue to contrast with the immaculate white of the walls. A light-toned wood was chosen for the floors, except for in the library-sitting room, finished in dark tones.

The main area of the flat is divided into the dining room, living room and kitchen, the latter partially concealed by a grey cubicle. From the living room, one enters the library-sitting room, outfitted with a spectacular set of galvanised steel shelves. Perhaps the most ingenious example of architectural wit, however, is to be found in the entry hall: a flight of wooden stairs leads to the spaces of the upper level. The desks and chalkboards of yesteryear, of course, have given way to a restrained, yet elegant selection of furnishings.

Though large windows paint every corner of the loft with natural light, this was seen as no reason not to strategically use high-design lamps.

Granite was chosen for the kitchen floor, in the tones of the loft's two predominant colours: white and grey.

Architect: Loof & Van Stigt

Location: Amsterdam, the Netherlands

Photographs: Guy Obijn

A wooden stair with a steel railing connects the entry hall with the upper level, housing the master bedroom, guest bedrooms, as well as an inviting terrace. ➤

 The kitchen was fitted into a grey cubicle, and to give it light and air several holes were opened in its ceiling.

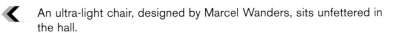 An ultra-light chair, designed by Marcel Wanders, sits unfettered in the hall.

In the foreground, the living room, furnished with a sofa and two white armchairs, as well as a unique coffee table with a set of wide wheels. In the background, the dining room and kitchen.

In the library-sitting room, complete with fireplace, one cannot help but breathe glamour. Might it have anything to do with the orange Rietveld chairs and the 85-bulb Rody Graumans lamp?

Imagination has no limits. Or have you seen cubic lamps with wheels before?

Wooden chairs and a wicker easy chair were chosen for the upper level's small terrace, a plant-lover's haven.

» Uninhibited

The owners of this loft, built in what was the storehouse of an old coffee roastery, were in the middle of divergent stylistic love-affairs when it came down to decorating their new home. As they were unwilling to forego any of these, they decided to combine them. The results are exquisite: the pedigree Cubist furniture, replete with pieces by Le Corbusier and Frank Lloyd Wright, unabashedly bumps elbows with antiques, such as an centenary Chinese chest, and other pieces of art deco. So that the building's origins wouldn't slip away forgotten, its old brick walls were kept intact, but painted white, as well as the arched shape of some of the windows.

To make the most of the available floor area, an upper level was built to make space for reading and a small terrace. The beauty of the system of beams and the columns that sustain them is accented by the play of light, and the unassuming ceiling, in contrast to the contemporary décor, establishes a unique overall balance. Such a welcoming, warm, and well-lit loft is proof positive that no detail was left to chance.

The iron fireplace was fitted into a pillar right behind the dining room table.

Warm-toned rugs of grand proportions are used to subtly define spaces.

Location: Antwerp, Belgium

Photographs: Guy Obijn

The black leather sofas, the wood floor and white walls make for a restful, tranquil reading area. ➤

In the foreground, the dining room. To the right, one can see the fireplace and to the left, an antique Chinese piece more than one hundred years old.

The entry is hidden behind a white partition and elevated on a wooden platform. The black leather chair was designed by Frank Lloyd Wright.

Dim light and white walls accentuate the straight, austere lines of the furniture.

 The living room, centred on two beige sofas and two coffee tables at floor level, is completely covered by the daunting wooden roof. Behind these one can see the dining room.

The kitchen is a statement in modernity and good taste. The stairs, combining wooden and metal elements, lead to the upper level.

Blue moon

As soon as he discovered architect Seth Stein's work, the owner of this flat knew that he wanted Stein on the job. Working with this loft, situated in an old office block in Fulham, Stein sought to create an undivided space of clean lines that would still, albeit through a different guise, reflect the original structure of the building.

A white bench, ingeniously running along the perimeter of the loft, was Stein's response to the client's desire for straight lines. Concrete beams in the ceiling were maintained, oak flooring compensating for the sensation of impassivity they produce. Wishing to avoid the colour white when painting the walls, a brilliant blue was chosen instead, which recurs in the décor. When it came to choosing furniture, the client wished to showcase his eclectic tastes, selecting everything from a red Rietveld chair to a blue velvet sofa taken from the Odeon cinemas and an original art deco sofa (refusing imitations) brought all the way from South Africa.

The master bedroom and the shower are separated from the common areas by a sliding door painted a brilliant blue.

The loft's overall ambivalence—whether it would serve as a place for rest, or a space to meet with friends—is what appealed most to the client.

Architect: Seth Stein

Location: Fulham, London, England

Photographs: Mathew Weinreb

From this perspective one can make out the straight lines that define the living room: the white partition separating it from the dining room and the concrete beams spanning the ceiling.

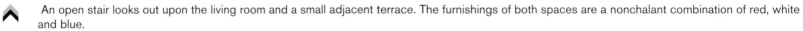

An open stair looks out upon the living room and a small adjacent terrace. The furnishings of both spaces are a nonchalant combination of red, white and blue.

A slit in the wall, serving as a headboard, adorns the bed with a subtle halo of light.

A panel of sanded glass separates the kitchen from the dining room.

A plinth of polished cement accommodates the bathtub, instilling the bathroom with a savage air.

» A trip to Venice

A quick glance at this loft and one would think he was in an Italian palazzo overlooking the Piazza San Marco. Nothing, however, could be further from the truth. This sumptuous dwelling is right in the heart of Amsterdam, occupying a 300-square-metre engine shed constructed in 1880. After its profound transformation, though, only a few beams and columns, painted a brilliant red and well-integrated into their surroundings, testify to the origins of this space.

This lofts' owner had no qualms whatsoever when it came to grouping classical art and antiques with contemporary pieces. The stylistic cocktail is unmistakable throughout the dwelling, whose spaces daringly fuse classicism and modernity. Likewise, there was no contention over the scheme of colours–the winning ensemble being a combination of blue and red. Nevertheless, the distribution of spaces is patently classical: a kitchen opens on to the dining room and living room, these distinguished primarily by unique floor treatments. Quite to the contrary, however, the library, bedrooms and bathroom are hidden behind curvilinear aluminium walls, the antithesis of classical.

The contrast between classical and modern is repeated over and again throughout the loft. An element of the provocateur, perhaps?

The materials used for the floor range from simple blue tile to polished wood planks, polished concrete and marble.

Architect: F.A. Schoen

Location: Amsterdam, the Netherlands

Photographs: Guy Obijn

The hall hints at the loft's predominant style: classical art, antiques, and large canvasses.

 The mural adorning the entry hall is a copy of a work by Italian artist Tiepolo.

In a corner of the library, brimming with art books, a grouped chair and table suggest that just maybe time has stopped.

Sliding doors allow the library to be isolated from the rest of the rooms.

The kitchen, in the centre of the loft, is an intense metallic blue. To the right: Classical elements, such as the mantelpiece and bust, and modern touches, like an abstract painting and shag carpet, intermingle in the living room.

Three vaguely industrial lamps contrast with the serving dishes, candlesticks, cut glass and silver resting atop the table.

Reflected in a mirror fitted with a bas-relief, gilded frame, one steals another glimpse of the living room, once again a combination of designer furniture and antiques.

A buddhist air

Who would have ever guessed that a block of offices built in the 1950s for #British Gas# would end up housing, exactly one half-century later, a collection of lofts designed by some of the world's most renowned architects, including John Pawson and Seth Stein? Lifschutz Davison began to remodel the building in 1997, thus beginning the conversion of this mammoth block of cement, re-baptised the Piper Building, into one of Fulham's few buildings of lofts.

Architect Ian Faithfull had a certain mantra in mind while he was designing the individual spaces of this loft: #rather than isolate, fuse#. The result is a series of spaces that interweave both from front to back and top to bottom. Crucial to achieving such continuity and fluidity was the use of glass banisters on the upper level. The clients' vast collection of art—brought back from numerous trips abroad—characterises the attractive, yet unpretentious décor, betraying a penchant for anything and everything Buddhist.

Passing through the living room one reaches a small terrace, one of the flat's hidden treasures.

The combination of quality materials, objets d'art and designer furniture is flawless.

Architect: Ian Faithfull

Location: Fulham, London, England

Photographs: Mathew Weinreb

The L-shaped, grey sofa designed by Woodgate looks out upon the terrace and, perpendicularly, faces a panoramic-screen television.

The master bedroom centres about a fireplace used to display various decorative pieces.

A reclinable Eames chair occupies a corner of the upper level.

Furniture to decorate the clients' office, adjacent to their painting studio, was chosen from a black and white palette. A psychedelic rug, inspired by designs from the 1960s, sprawls in the centre of the room.

Views from the upper level to the living room. A robust white wooden shelf, brimming with art objects, separates this space from the kitchen.

The upper level, left completely open to the living room, serves as the flat's leisure centre: proof of this are the billiards table, guitar, saxophone and chessboard.

The bed, decorated simply but without sacrificing elegance, lies in the centre of the bedroom.

The bathroom floor and walls are of Portuguese limestone. The sink pedestal is glass and the washbasin, stainless steel.

The hearth is the centre of attention in the living room, capturing the eye with a sleek metal chimney which rises to the ceiling.

» Aesthetic brutality

The directions architect Nicolas Vanderhaeghen were given to remodel a loft looking out on Antwerp's port were clear: its spaces had to both combine the atmosphere of an artist's studio with elements of aesthetic brutalism, and flow in and out of one another effortlessly. A 625-square-metre space, left after the fusion of the two lofts that occupied the top floor of an old granary, were enough for Vanderhaegen to achieve that goal and accomplish much more.

The key to its rebirth was finding transparency through the play of light and the complicity of the white-painted brick walls. One of the sources of natural light is the terrace, which was built to partially cover the living room and is accessed via a glass bridge. The first floor was reserved for various sitting rooms, the dining room, kitchen and bathroom while the second floor was given over to bedroom and an office. Some areas of the loft even recall the walls of a contemporary art gallery or an artist's studio, one of the client's pursuits. African sculptures, baroque mirrors and vaguely cinematic knickknacks—that would make a collector's mouth water—are to be found throughout the loft. It is difficult to say whether the lighting or the furniture takes the prize for best design—without a doubt the end result is stunning.

The immensity of the space forced the architect to install metal stairs at each end of the loft to ease access to the upper level.

Iron columns and beams are so well integrated they seem to be merely decoration, even though their initial function was to sustain the structure of the building.

Architect: Nicolas Vanderhaeghen

Location: Antwerp, Belgium

Photographs: Guy Obijn

A Marilyn Monroe figurine—à la *Seven-year Itch*—on display in the living room, hints at the owner's rather outlandish tastes.

A view of one of the sitting rooms, fitted with dark-hued furniture and large works of art. To the right: a glass catwalk was built adjacent to the other living room, decorated in white, beneath which were hung photographs.

A circular opening, imitating the porthole of a ship, links the dining room with the kitchen.

The library also has white leather sofas and chairs. The metal stairs lead to the office.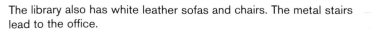

 The decoration based around the original iron beams was also extended to the bathroom, lined in blue granite.

Leopard skin was chosen to upholster the chairs and bed set in the master bedroom. Closets were built into the walls.

The dining room, presided over by an impressive Cubist painting, is limited to a robust wooden table and ten stuffed chairs in white. Noteworthy too is the lamp, hanging from the iron beams that span the loft.

Elegance in white

Over the years, a 1930s Clerkenwell building that had originally housed a printing press evolved into the perfect site to build lofts. One of the first storeys to be rehabilitated was the attic, whose strange floor plan traces a letter Z. Architect Malcolm Crayton let his imagination run wild, and under the premise of not aligning any two elements, he procured that the space breathe elegance without being overly academic. To achieve this, he wove together a succession of subordinate spaces, interconnecting them using a system of sliding panels that would allow the tenant to separate and join areas as he liked. To further accentuate this quality, he enclosed the dining room and living room—which share one wing of the loft—between white columns. Atop the kitchen, he built an open platform hemmed in by glass-panelled railings, all around which enormous cabinets provide space for all sorts of possessions.

The loft's large windows afford breathtaking vistas of the city and flood its rooms with natural light. Austere furniture was chosen to decorate the loft, harmonising perfectly with the pristine white of the walls.

Electric heating was installed behind the skirting board in all the rooms to avoid the presence of radiators.

To eschew chaos*, the architect devised a system of cabinets and drawers that hide everything from electrical appliances to televisions, stereos and a mini-bar.

Architect: Malcolm Crayton (Form Architects)

Location: Clerkenwell, London, England

Photographs: Mathew Weinreb

The dining room and living room, with excellent views north to London, occupy the central part of the loft.

The kitchen units delimit the entrance to the spacious common area. To take advantage of this space a second level was constructed above this.

Glass and limestone predominate in the bathroom. A fibre-optic fixture illuminates the shower.

 The master bedroom is a set of volumes, the different intensities of light imparting an unique nuance to each one.

The clean lines of the kitchen mesh perfectly into the structure of the loft.

Walls with history

The walls of the De Appel warehouse mask many years of history. Though it makes its first mention in the Amsterdam town archives in 1711, historians place its construction at somewhere around 1660. Its current owner, an estate agent, purchased it in 1971 from the Amsterdam Tobacco Company in a miserable state of repair. Towards the end of the 1990s, he decided to rehabilitate it and make it into his home. Thus he began the painstaking task of restoring the extant elements to their original splendour: wooden beams were repaired and painted, along with the brick walls and parts of the wood floor. Loading bays, as well as openings for ventilation, were kept intact.

The distribution of spaces was elaborately studied and finally the common areas were nestled together on the ground floor and personal spaces, such as the bedrooms, library and office, on the upper level. Solid wooden pieces and straight lines characterise the décor, in addition to small objets d'art and sculptures that reveal the client's philanthropy.

In contrast to other warehouses in the area, which were typically divided in two, De Appel maintains it original length of 30 metres.

The client's passion for art is most evident: an eclectic array of paintings hangs in each of the rooms.

The spaces of the dwelling were easily adapted to fit them to the original structure of the warehouse. The white brick walls contrasts sharply with the wooden beams of the ceiling, painted black.

Location: Amsterdam, the Netherlands

Photographs: Jo Jetten

Two grey sofas and the hearth, with its unique pyramidal hood, fill the living room with a welcoming air. In lieu of a coffee table, small end tables store books and magazines. To the right: a spacious work area.

The loft, as it was thirty years ago when the current owner purchased it.

Here, wooden stairs lead to the library and the master bedroom, directly atop the area occupied by the dining room.

Enormous wooden beams cross the ceiling of the simply-decorated bedroom. To the right: a general view of the dining room, situated in the centre of the old warehouse. The kitchen is hidden behind the white wall.

An antique chest of drawers is caught reflected in the bedroom mirror, right beside a Japanese-style lamp.

The kitchen was finished in a rustic style—though somewhat out of character with the rest of loft—pots and pans rest, nonchalant, in plain view.

A designer garden

Architect Nigel Smith and his son share this impeccable loft, which occupies the top floor of a factory built in the 1930s near a railway station. Its remarkable location yields it with panoramic views of London and natural light thanks to the enormous windows, which, in some places, even come to replace walls. Paying homage to the original structure of the building, some of its brick walls were maintained; nevertheless, others, as well as the beams and columns, were clad in concrete—its coarse aspect softened by the luminous wood floor. Spaces were distributed classically, with the dining room and living room fused into one. A small office was located in the other wing, while the bedrooms and baths were hidden from the common areas.

Classic twentieth-century designs played an important role in the choice of décor. This explains the profusion of Eames originals (the living room lamp, dining room sofa and chairs), in addition to pieces by Jean Rison (the living room chairs), and Florence Knoll (the oval dining room table). To provide storage for belongings, the walls of one of the bedrooms were transformed into deep closets and the ceiling lowered to make room for a loft space.

The kitchen, painted an intense indigo blue, is set apart by its concrete countertop into which fits the sink.

The strategic arrangement of furniture suggests that its aim had been to create the sensation of being in a sculpture garden.

A central heating system was installed beneath the floor to avoid cluttering the loft with radiators.

Architect: Nigel Smith

Location: London, England

Photographs: Mathew Weinreb

Since the walls were already occupied by dressers, the bed and its headboard were placed in the centre of the room.

An immense refrigerator, leaping out from the blue tile walls in unmistakably American fashion, is the most striking kitchen appliance.

Loft Crepain

Architect Jo Crepain decided to establish his studio and home in an industrial warehouse built at the beginning of the last century. He completely restored the building, an antique five-storey rectangular warehouse, deliberately maintaining original structures. Windows that had been bricked over were reopened and the vaulting repaired for the space to recover its primitive air. Openings and doors that had been cut into the building at a later time were eliminated.

The programme includes two distinct spaces. One side is his home with a room to house his art collection, a terrace, master bedroom, guest bedroom and studio. Office space for some 40 people was carved out of the other side of the building, complete with a conference room, screening room and dining area. Outside, trees were planted to make a courtyard and a small, 10-space car park was opened after the demolition of an office building situated behind the warehouse.

Living space extends across the upper two floors of the building. Its location grants it spectacular panoramic views of the city, with the spire of Antwerp's cathedral acting as a magnificent focal point.

The main living room is flooded with light thanks to ample lateral and frontal windows. It provided the perfect space for the library and the owners' art collection, and also opens prominently—as they had wished—on to the terrace, which faces west and looks back in on the dwelling through immense sliding glass doors.

The arrangement of the living room furniture allows the room to take full advantage of the natural light coming in from the terraces and lateral windows.

A concrete well was built in the space occupied by the old industrial service lift to make room for a lift and stair, in addition to plumbing and electrical wiring.

The exterior windows and doors are crafted in metal with double glazing for insulation.

Architect: Jo Crepain

Location: Antwerp, Belgium

Photographs: Ludo Noel, Jan Verlinde

The building is located a few steps away from the river Scheldt. Its position above the banks of the river grants privileged views of the city from the terrace

Cold colours, like grey, blue and white are the primary tones in the décor. Red brushstrokes add contrast and highlight particular elements of the loft.

The loft's austere materials are conducive to calm and relaxation while at the same time preserving the industrial air of an antique warehouse.

The arched brick vaulting was restored to its original appearance.
Eight wrought iron columns divide the space.

The bedrooms are delimited by sliding doors and panels, which, without closing the rooms off, allow them to maintain privacy.

The kitchen centres on an enormous elongated worktable. One of its ends is fitted out to serve as a dining room table.

> Dovetailed spaces

This loft, in London's northern reaches, looks out upon an industrial landscape of railways and factories. This aspect, however, presented no problem to its owner, American photographer David Bailey, who already owned a loft in Tribeca, one of the few parts of Manhattan with extant reminders of an industrial past. Situated in an antique florist's warehouse built in the 1930s, the building had been divided into independent spaces at the end of the 1990s to be developed into luxury apartments.

In this loft in particular, the raw character of concrete was combined to full effect with the original brick structure, although some of these walls were replaced with glass panels to take maximum advantage of natural light. This contemporary touch was seconded by the construction of a cubicle, concealing an office, in glass block. A white cube forms the central focus of the loft, containing the kitchen, wrought in granite and steel, a fourth bathroom and an area destined for use as display space. Nestled around it are the living room and dining room. In both of these the client opted for a very strict décor, combining black leather and steel. A reading area was placed in the far end, along with both bedrooms and the remaining bathrooms.

To keep the common areas neat and tidy, the architect designed large closets and camouflaged them behind secret doors.

Heaters were installed beneath the parquet flooring, thus eliminating the need to install radiators on the walls.

Location: London, England

Photographs: Mathew Weinreb

The living room décor's dark tones are compensated for by the ruddy tones of the wood floor. >

This welcoming corner to read, complete with fireplace, opens directly on to the terrace.

Austerity is the word best suiting the bathroom, which is reflected in its white fittings, glass doors and absence of superfluous objects.

The sober and elegant master bedroom—which uses glass block in one section of its wall—has its own bathroom.

> Noah's ark

The restless traveller's spirit of the owners of this loft, which occupies the top floor and immense attic of what had been a primary school, makes itself felt in every corner. A good part of this globetrotting atmosphere is owed to the extensive collection of photographs—taken on trips abroad—found throughout the house. Its décor, an assortment of animal motifs, makes this loft a veritable Noah's Ark.

On the lower level, profusely lit by a unique series of arching windows, the kitchen—with all its utensils in plain sight—fuses into the dining room. Here black and white tiles were judiciously combined on the floor to contrast with the ruddy wooden chairs and table. A simple white wooden stair leads to the attic, whose impressive wooden timbers imitate the hull of a ship. The living room and bedroom share the largest part of this space, its original chestnut floor beautifully restored. Both are decorated in white, and the collection of photographs and objects brought back from all over the world heighten the sense of adventure that this dwelling is sure to awaken in the visitor. Out of one corner, decorated with a striking rug, a niche was carved to place a piano.

Animals, each in its own particular way, were a source of inspiration for the décor: turtles, crocodiles, fish, hedgehogs, elephants, lions, snails…

Several skylights were opened in the attic to allow more natural light to filter in.

Location: Amsterdam, the Netherlands

Photographs: Diederik van der Mieden

A spectacular view of the attic, whose roof was built to imitate the hull of a ship.

The kitchen and dining room are integrated into one single area, remarkable for the checkerboard colours of the floor and the unique arched windows. A large rectangular table is flanked by chairs designed by Thoet, and a wooden staircase ascends to the attic.

One corner of the kitchen shows off a Klaas Gubbels canvas as well as works by other artists.

Another perspective of the living room, brimming with souvenirs from trips abroad. To the right: the bedroom occupies a portion of the upper level right across from the living room. A skylight guarantees ample natural light.

Silver candlesticks, glass bottles, and even jars of jam rest atop the table. In the kitchen, everyday things are in view, while wooden and glass display cases housing objets d'art organise the dining room.

The bathtub was ingeniously hidden behind two doors made to look like closets.